James Fraser Gluck

A Little Guide to Niagara Falls

James Fraser Gluck

A Little Guide to Niagara Falls

ISBN/EAN: 9783743442795

Manufactured in Europe, USA, Canada, Australia, Japa

Cover: Foto ©Andreas Hilbeck / pixelio.de

Manufactured and distributed by brebook publishing software
(www.brebook.com)

James Fraser Gluck

A Little Guide to Niagara Falls

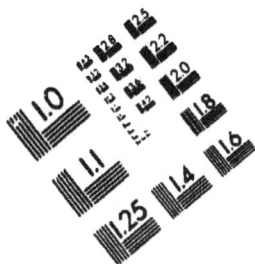

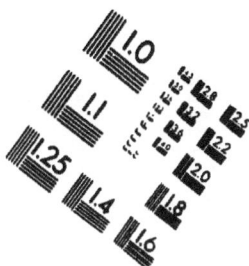

**IMAGE EVALUATION
TEST TARGET (MT-3)**

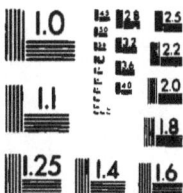

Photographic
Sciences
Corporation

23 WEST MAIN STREET
WEBSTER, N.Y. 14580
(716) 872-4503

Technical and Bibliographic Notes/Notes techniques et bibliographiques

The Institute has attempted to obtain the best original copy available for filming. Features of this copy which may be bibliographically unique, which may alter any of the images in the reproduction, or which may significantly change the usual method of filming, are checked below.

L'Institut a microfilmé le meilleur exemplaire qu'il lui a été possible de se procurer. Les détails de cet exemplaire qui sont peut-être uniques du point de vue bibliographique, qui peuvent modifier une image reproduite, ou qui peuvent exiger une modification dans la méthode normale de filmage sont indiqués ci-dessous.

[X] Coloured covers/
Couverture de couleur

[ ] Covers damaged/
Couverture endommagée

[ ] Covers restored and/or laminated/
Couverture restaurée et/ou pelliculée

[ ] Cover title missing/
Le titre de couverture manque

[ ] Coloured maps/
Cartes géographiques en couleur

[ ] Coloured ink (i.e. other than blue or black)/
Encre de couleur (i.e. autre que bleue ou noire)

[ ] Coloured plates and/or illustrations/
Planches et/ou illustrations en couleur

[ ] Bound with other material/
Relié avec d'autres documents

[X] Tight binding may cause shadows or distortion along interior margin/
La reliure serrée peut causer de l'ombre ou de la distortion le long de la marge intérieure

[ ] Blank leaves added during restoration may appear within the text. Whenever possible, these have been omitted from filming/
Il se peut que certaines pages blanches ajoutées lors d'une restauration apparaissent dans le texte, mais, lorsque cela était possible, ces pages n'ont pas été filmées.

[ ] Additional comments:/
Commentaires supplémentaires:

[ ] Coloured pages/
Pages de couleur

[X] Pages damaged/
Pages endommagées

[ ] Pages restored and/or laminated/
Pages restaurées et/ou pelliculées

[ ] Pages discoloured, stained or foxed/
Pages décolorées, tachetées ou piquées

[ ] Pages detached/
Pages détachées

[ ] Showthrough/
Transparence

[ ] Quality of print varies/
Qualité inégale de l'impression

[ ] Includes supplementary material/
Comprend du matériel supplémentaire

[ ] Only edition available/
Seule édition disponible

[ ] Pages wholly or partially obscured by errata slips, tissues, etc., have been refilmed to ensure the best possible image/
Les pages totalement ou partiellement obscurcies par un feuillet d'errata, une pelure, etc., ont été filmées à nouveau de façon à obtenir la meilleure image possible.

The copy filmed here has been reproduced thanks
to the generosity of:

Library of Congress
Photoduplication Service

The images appearing here are the best quality
possible considering the condition and legibility
of the original copy and in keeping with the
filming contract specifications.

Original copies in printed paper covers are filmed
beginning with the front cover and ending on
the last page with a printed or illustrated impression, or the back cover when appropriate. All
other original copies are filmed beginning on the
first page with a printed or illustrated impression, and ending on the last page with a printed
or illustrated impression.

The last recorded frame on each microfiche
shall contain the symbol →► (meaning "CON-
TINUED"), or the symbol ▽ (meaning "END"),
whichever applies.

Maps, plates, charts, etc., may be filmed at
different reduction ratios. Those too large to be
entirely included in one exposure are filmed
beginning in the upper left hand corner, left to
right and top to bottom, as many frames as
required. The following diagrams illustrate the
method:

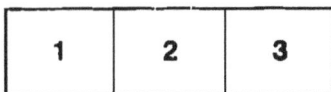

L'exemplaire filmé fut reproduit grâce à la
générosité de:

Library of Congress
Photoduplication Service

Les images suivantes ont été reproduites avec le
plus grand soin, compte tenu de la condition et
de la netteté de l'exemplaire filmé, et en
conformité avec les conditions du contrat de
filmage.

Les exemplaires originaux dont la couverture en
papier est imprimée sont filmés en commençant
par le premier plat et en terminant soit par la
dernière page qui comporte une empreinte
d'impression ou d'illustration, soit par le second
plat, selon le cas. Tous les autres exemplaires
originaux sont filmés en commençant par la
première page qui comporte une empreinte
d'impression ou d'illustration et en terminant par
la dernière page qui comporte une telle
empreinte.

Un des symboles suivants apparaîtra sur la
dernière image de chaque microfiche, selon le
cas: le symbole →► signifie "A SUIVRE", le
symbole ▽ signifie "FIN".

Les cartes, planches, tableaux, etc., peuvent être
filmés à des taux de réduction différents.
Lorsque le document est trop grand pour être
reproduit en un seul cliché, il est filmé à partir
de l'angle supérieur gauche, de gauche à droite,
et de haut en bas, en prenant le nombre
d'images nécessaire. Les diagrammes suivants
illustrent la méthode.

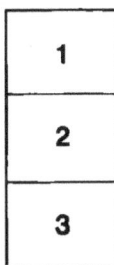

1	2	3

1
2
3

A Little Guide to
Niagara Falls

HORSE SHOE FALLS FROM GOAT ISLAND

A

LITTLE GUIDE

TO

NIAGARA FALLS

CONTAINING

/ Brief Description of the Principal Points of Interest,
How Best to Reach Them, Their Leading
Characteristics, etc., Together with
the Prices Charged for Guides.
Carriages, and Conveni-
ences at each Place,

AND A

PROGRAM FOR A TWO WEEKS' VISIT,

BY

AN OLD RESIDENT.

Jas. Fraser Gluck

*"Niagara Falls is the crowning glory of New York
State, and the highest distinction of the American Con-
tinent."*

MATTHEWS, NORTHRUP & CO.
BUFFALO AND NEW YORK.
1890.

F 127
N3G5

INDEX.

Guide Map of
NIAGARA
FALLS

A

LITTLE GUIDE

in

NIAGARA FALLS.

Reader, you are now at Niagara Falls. You have read about it. You have seen pictures of it. You have been asked if you have visited it. You have longed to behold it. You are here.

Will it, indeed, seem to you to be what so many great minds have pronounced it, " The most beautiful sight in the world ? " Will it seem worthy of your admiration, your reverence and your love ? Believe me, dear reader, that will depend very largely upon the *tone* and *temper* — the *thoughts* with which you approach it. If you would know the real elements of its beauty, the thoughts it has excited in the minds of many distinguished men and women, you will not regret procuring at the hotels at Niagara — either at the SPENCER HOUSE or at the INTERNATIONAL HOTEL— the little pamphlet entitled, " Introduction to Niagara Falls." The extracts there given, will, I hope, do much to place you in the right *mood* to really see and to study Niagara. The reading of that pamphlet, will, I believe, do away with a flood of erroneous ideas, You will begin to appreciate how utterly futile and absurd it is to attempt to "do" Niagara in a few hours or a day. How ignominious and contemptible a proceeding it is to drive hurriedly in and about these sacred precincts in a hack.

ARRIVAL AT
NIAGARA.

You will resolutely close your ears to all offers to "drive you around it" for a small sum. You will seat yourself at the hotel until you have carefully perused this pamphlet, and then, and not until then, start out to get your first glimpse of Niagara. May it be but one of a great number! May it be your experience, as it has been mine, that the more you see it the more grand, majestic, and surpassingly beautiful it will seem, and the more ardently you will desire not to pass a day, but weeks and months on this enchanted ground.

Why, if this is so, is it that so many people hurry in their visit to Niagara? The reason is this, Where there is one person who really desires to see Niagara, there are hundreds who simply desire to *say* they have seen it. These are they who come in the morning and go away at noon — who glance at Niagara as if that one look could give them any just conception of its grandeur and beauty, and who never even have a single sensation of awe, admiration, or astonishment; who jump into carriages, gabble on the way, chatter on the brink of the awful cataract, drive rapidly to the noise of their own voices, through its majestic woods — fit spots for sweet and solemn thoughts — listen to some garbled tales of horror, told by an ignorant driver, keep on the move all day, and depart — poor, foolish souls! — imagining they have seen Niagara! They have never even commenced to comprehend the first element of its beauty.

Let this not be your temper, your spirit, your method of viewing Niagara. Come to it resolved to make its beauty part of your own mental self, its grandeur and majesty part of the current of your thought. Let its great and glorious pictures be so etched on your memory by repeated visits, that these will shine forever lighted up by the sunlight of remembrance, in the gallery of your choicest mental treasures. Then Niagara will be to you an inspiration, a blessed recollection, a theme of serious comment, and — recalling

8

its loveliness, its awful majesty, its exquisite beauty — your thoughts will be insensibly and repeatedly led to the Eternal Spirit, the Divine Artist, whose work this is.

I assume now, that, arriving in the evening, let us say, you will select as your hotel either the Spencer House — directly opposite the New York Central Station — or the International Hotel — the nearest hotel to the Falls, and three blocks from the New York Central station. Thoroughly refreshed by a good night's sleep and an excellent breakfast, you begin your first day at Niagara. From the Spencer House you step out on the front piazza, turn to your left and walk directly down the street three blocks to the Falls. You cannot miss your way. If you are at the International, step out of the rear of the office on to the piazza and the Rapids, Goat Island, and Prospect Park are in full view. Walk down the lawn and you will see the sidewalk leading to the Falls. Follow that and you find yourself at Prospect Park — entirely free — where, from Prospect Point you obtain your first full view of the great Falls, as well as a general survey of the various points of view and objects of interest.

FIRST GENERAL VIEW OF FALLS.

Directly in front of you are the Falls. Upon your left, the bridge leading to Goat Island, the Goat Island group, the Upper Rapids. To your right is the inclined stairway leading to the foot of the American Falls, and from which you start on a most enjoyable trip on the little steamer "Maid of the Mist," which takes you up to the very foot of the Horseshoe Falls. Further to the right you see the new Suspension Bridge leading to Canada, and then back upon the left, on the Canadian side, you see the road winding along the river bank past Table Rock to the edge of the Canadian Falls, and thence through the delightful Queen Victoria Park, also free; thence the road leads up to the Dufferin Isles, the most exquisitely beautiful and retired spot about

Niagara; passing these, the road winds up the river
—one of the most lovely drives in the world. Cast-
ing your eyes back now to the right, below the upper
Suspension Bridge, you catch sight of the road winding
down the side of the river, conducting you to the Whirlpool and Whirlpool Rapids, and various other points
of interest to be hereafter described.

Now you have your bearings. You can begin to see
Niagara now, if you will. You are now at Prospect
Park, with its comfortable seats, its venerable trees, its
delightful views—all of which are yours without price
or fee. The State of New York paid over a million
dollars to enable you to enjoy this privilege. Yours is
the estate if you will only use it.

Why deprive yourself of sufficient time to enjoy its
beauty?

Observe the changing glories of the great cataract.
Note the magnificent cloud-forms above the Falls, the
ever-varying shapes which the rushing rapids assume,
the effects of the sunlight on the rising spray, transform-
ing its cold mists into rainbow colors, shifting, rising and
falling in eternal motion. Rest quietly under these venerable trees and let the sight become etched upon your
soul—there to remain a picture of beauty and of
power, in after years one of your choicest possessions.
The time will seem all too short when your watch will
inform you it is time to return to the hotel to enjoy the
noon-day meal, and to give the surfeited imagination
and exhausted vision an opportunity to recover their
full force to appreciate new sights of beauty.

If during the remainder of the day you desire to
rest, or to enjoy the Rapids from a distance—lunch
leisurely and watch the Falls from the International
piazza; if you desire to acquire information relating to
the historical incidents connected with Niagara, a volume on this subject will be furnished you, which you
can read at your leisure on the cool and shady piazzas
of either Hotel.

ICE BRIDGE AND AMERICAN FALLS

Should you desire to drive, you can procure a carriage at the Hotel, or a van in the Prospect Park, to go about Goat Island for the morning or afternoon, allowing you ample time to alight and acquaint yourself with the location of the various places of interest which you really visit later *on foot*, to truly appreciate. The highest price you should pay for the carriage is two dollars for your party, and you can possibly get it cheaper by making a special bargain. The price of a seat in one of the vans is twenty-five cents per person.

But — let me again repeat — if you start to *walk* at any time, on this or any other trip, do not, *under any consideration*, allow yourself to be persuaded by some persistent hackman — utterly irresponsible and sometimes thoroughly dangerous, not even hesitating at highway robbery — to *be "taken around to see everything" for one or two dollars!* You will end by being thoroughly tired, surfeited and discontented, dissatisfied with yourself and Niagara, confused by its sights and sounds, and anxious to depart.

WALK ABOUT GOAT ISLAND.

Let us assume, then, that you will start on the *second* day of your visit for a walk or drive about Goat Island — that loveliest jewel in fair Niagara's crown. Passing over the first bridge you are upon Bath Island, thence you pass over the second bridge and are upon Goat Island. Turn now to the right and pass along one of the loveliest walks in the world until you come to a point overlooking the American Falls, and where there is a staircase winding down the bank to a bridge, passing to a small but lovely island. This is Luna Island, and it is from this point that one has the finest view of that dream of loveliness, the rainbow by moonlight, or as it is usually called, the Lunar bow. Observe the view, in order to return and study it at your leisure again. Retrace your steps up the stair-case, and proceed along the river bank until the house is reached surmounted by the sign "Cave of the Winds." Passing

through this house the visitor reaches the bottom of
the bank by a winding stair-case, thence along the
bank leading to that, perhaps, most magnificent and
awful of all scenes at Niagara, the Cave of the Winds.
A charge is made for this trip — one dollar per person,
including in this charge a guide and a dress. The trip
is absolutely safe. No one has ever been lost, and it
is inconceivably grand. The visitor passes directly behind the Falls — and nowhere else can one realize the
resistless terrible force and power there is in the fall of
those apparently peaceful waters gliding smoothly and
swiftly to the brink. Noting the spot to return to it
again and visit this wonderful cave, continue along
the island-walk until there is a break in the foliage and
a clear view; stop now, and look over this precipice.
You begin to realize the immense height which separ-
ates you from the waters below. It is an impressive
and terrible scene, and it is not well to linger here long,
lest dizziness supervene.

Thence continue along the walk until the foliage
permits you to obtain a view of the Canadian Falls —
called the Great Crescent or Horseshoe Falls. Proceed down the fine staircase leading out over the
bridge to the edge of the Falls. This point is called
Terrapin Rocks, and upon it was formerly situated the
Terrapin Tower. Confess, now, that the view you have
of the entire Falls is one worth coming a thousand
miles to see. How it changes during the day! how
beauti'l in the morning! how magnificent in the full
noontide! how awful in the rays of the setting sun!
Day after day, and night after night, these great floods
descend — with no confusion or tumult, but ever-flow-
ing, resistless, terrible as fate itself. Glance at the
tremendous volume of waters with their hue of deep
emerald. Notice the lashed waves beneath on which
the little steamer, the " Maid of the Mist," with its
load of precious freight, rides like a little toy-boat in
safety.

Returning to the bank above, and turning to the right, follow the path through delightful forest walks up to the Three Sister Islands — visions of beauty and of grace which it is useless to attempt to describe. Here are charming little spots, cool and shady retreats in summer heat; here are dainty cascades with ten thousand various shades of color and shapes of beauty; here, as you sit on the third Sister Island, the wild onrushing rapids seem to descend from the skies, and every vestige of civilization has completely disappeared.

You are in the very presence of terrible, yet beautiful Nature. The man who cannot for hours sit here and find unceasing delight in the contemplation of this truly beautiful sight, may well suspect that he does not properly comprehend the Spirit that speaks to man through the multitudinous sounds of Nature.

Returning once more to the Goat Island shore, continue your walk to the right to the upper end of the island. How complete the change! How utterly impossible it is to realize that so short a distance below the great Falls exists! How placid and quiet the river seems — how melodious and soothing its gentle ripple and murmur! Of all spots about Niagara this is one of the most attractive, and, after lingering here, you may continue your walk back to the Island bridge, stopping on your way at the Spring below the bank to enjoy a cup of the purest water, and watching from your shady retreat, amid the embowering trees, the glittering waves, the tossing shapes, the wild magnificence of the Rapids. In this part of Niagara alone you will find more enchanting bowers of grace and beauty than in all the glens of Watkins and Havana. Continuing your walk, you reach the spot from which you started.

Usually you should visit the Goat Island Group on foot in the morning; the foliage is fresher and brighter, and at every one of the spots we have alluded to half a day may profitably be passed. Leading through the Island are forest walks to the Terrapin Rocks and the Three Sister Islands, absolutely quiet nooks in the very recesses of the primitive forest where you may walk and linger for hours undisturbed, with care and business-tumult apparently ten thousand miles away. The birds are singing all about you; the squirrels come and play at your feet; many new kinds of wild flowers bloom there; the sunlight falls on a carpet of soft moss and of dainty ferns — while over your head arch the forest boughs and the great sky, pure and clear, unsullied by the city's smoke and dust.

Yet all this time you have seen and studied only the beauties of one island at Niagara; selected because it is a fair illustration of many, many other spots. Yet creatures having the form and general appearance of rational human beings actually attempt to "do all Niagara" in a *day !*

It may not be uninteresting in this connection for the visitor to read Charles Dudley Warner's description of the Goat Island walk, as given in his delightful work, " Their Pilgrimage." Here it is:

" The walk around Goat Island is probably unsurpassed in the world for wonder and beauty. The Americans have every reason to be satisfied with their share of the fall. They get nowhere one single grand view like that from the Canada side, but infinitely the deepest impression of majesty and power is obtained on Goat Island. There the spectator is in the midst of the war of Nature. From the point over the Horseshoe Fall, our friends — speaking not much, but more and more deeply moved — strolled along the lovely forest, in a rural solemnity, in a local calm, almost a seclusion, except for the ever present shuddering roar in the air. On the shore above the Horseshoe, they first comprehended the breadth, the great sweep of the

; through the
ocks and the
s in the very
ou may walk
re and busi-
away. The
uirrels come
wild flowers
arpet of soft
· your head
ty, pure and
ist.

died only the
I because it is
spots. Yet
ppearance of
i to "do all

onnection for
ier's desc.ip-
his delightful

bably unsur-
eauty. The
ed with their
single grand
infinitely the
r is obtained
in the midst
ir the Horse-
ich, but more
g the lovely
:lm, almost a
iddering roar
rseshoe, they
sweep of the

rapids, the white crests of the waves ever coming out
from under a black, lowering sky. All the foreground
was in bright sunlight, dancing, sparkling, leaping, hurrying on, converging to the angle where the water becomes
a deep emerald, at the brink and plunge. The rapids
above are a series of shelves, bristling with jutting
rocks and lodged stumps of trees, and the wildness of
the scene is intensified by the rugged fringe of ever-
green on the opposite shore. Over the whole island,
the mist rising from the caldron, drifts in a spray when
the wind is favorable. But on this day the forest was
bright and cheerful, and as the strollers went farther
away from the great fall, the beauty of the scene began
to steal away its terror, the roar was still dominant,
but far off and softened, and did not crush the ear.
The triple islands, the Three Sisters, in their picturesque
wildness, appeared like playful freaks of Nature in a
momentary relaxation of the savage mood. Here is
the finest view of the river. To one standing on the
outmost island, the great flood seems tumbling out of
the sky. They continued along the bank of the river,
where the shallow stream races by headlong, but close
to the edges are numerous eddies, and places where
one might step in and not be swept away. At length
they reach the point where the river divides, and the
water stands for an instant almost still, hesitating
whether to take the Canadian or the American plunge.
Out a little way from the shore the waves leap and
tumble, and the two currents are like race-horses,
parted on two ways to the goal. Just at this point the
water swirls and lingers, having lost all its fierceness
and haste, and spreads itself out placidly, dimpling in
the sun. It may be a treacherous pause, this water
may be as cruel as that which rages below, and exults
in catching a boat or a man and bounding with the
victim over the cataract. But the calm was very grate-
ful to the stunned and buffeted visitors. Upon their
jarred nerves it was like the peace of God."

Let us assume you have passed your first day at Niagara in this general visit to Prospect Park and Goat Island. You have now, as it were, a bird's-eye view of the American side. Let us again on

TUESDAY

proceed to *study* this magnificent masterpiece of Nature. Starting again on Prospect Point, observe more carefully the scene. And hereafter, in the descriptions given, unless otherwise indicated, I use the words of the venerable man of whom I made mention in the little pamphlet "Introduction to Niagara." To him be all the praise of which they are worthy. Of this scene he says : — The river rolls by in the sunlight like a ruffled sea of silver, two hundred feet beneath the cliff from which you look down, bounded on either side by huge frowning walls of **VIEW FROM** limestone, crested by fair fields, **PROSPECT PARK,** and clustering forest trees, stretching away in the distance. The agitated and heaving abyss, the clouds of rising spray, the flashing snowy sheet hanging between sea and sky, the dark cliffs and islands that bound and divide them, the ocean of tumbling waters that seem sporting above and beyond the precipice, and come dancing over the cataract to the music of its everlasting roar, together form a scene, compared to which the ruins of Balbec or Palmyra, the Pyramids of Egypt, or the temples of Greece and Rome, are but the toys and foot-balls of time.

The best view of the Falls, on the American side, is from this point. Table Rock, the Horseshoe Fall Goat Island, the Central Fall, the American Fall, the rapids and islands above, and the abyss and river below, are all within sight ; but of the Horseshoe Fall the view is distant and partial. In fact, there is no complete view of the cataract on the American side. From

16

first day at
et Park and
, a bird's-eye
on

piece of Na-
observe more
e descriptions
the words of
ention in the
" To him he
Of this scene
sunlight like
beneath the
led on either
ning walls of
by fair fields,
forest trees,
the distance.
ouds of rising
between sea
at bound and
ers that seem
ce, and come
of its everlast-
to which the
s of Egypt, or
the ..ys and

merican side.
orseshoe Fall
rican Fall, th'
yss and rive.
lorseshoe Fa'
ere is no com-
n side. From

the opposite shore only, can Niagara be seen in all its parts, and in all its sublime majesty, at a single glance. But that one view, grand and overwhelming as it confessedly is, is almost the only one on the Canada shore. There are, it is true, many modifications of it, depending upon the points from which it is observed; but it is still the same in all its leading features, and has a strange oneness about it, that awes even more than it interests. The eye and the mind, pained by its transcendant vastness and sublimity, can scarcely dwell upon it without some interval of repose.

On the American side, on the contrary, while there is no one view of the cataract so grand and perfect, there are many of different parts, each exceedingly beautiful and impressive; and such a variety of river and forest scenery, that the attention is diverted from one object to another,— something new and fresh is presented at every turn, the eye is delighted, the mind excited by a constant succession of pleasing and august appearances,— and thus a delicious interest is kept up, which seems to while away the hours; and while lovely and striking images are fast crowding upon the eye and mind, they are both, as it were, refreshed and renovated by novelty and change.

From Prospect Point, having looked at the glorious scene as long as you choose, advance to the very brink of the cataract at Prospect Place. Here, standing on a secure platform, you can look directly down at the awful depths; the huge blocks of stone, the rock-dashed spray and foam, the shivering sheet, and the heaving abyss, and up at the Falls, and particularly the American cascade, of which you have a capital view, though not the best.

The American Fall is characterized by an irregularity that gives it a wild and singular beauty. The outline is far projecting and deeply indented, yet with no very abrupt transitions, and certainly no monotonous parallels. The water flows over it in a broad billowy

17

stream, and is thrown out by craggy points in a hundred places, so that it passes down in a glorious snow-
white drapery, wreathing into graceful fleecy folds,
and possessing so much variety with so complete a
unity, that it not only awes but delights, and you
almost forget its immensity in the contemplation of its
beauty. Near the shore, where the water is shallow,
the stream ripples along pure and clear as crystal, and
falls from the brink in a shower of sparkling brilliancy.
Large rocks lay piled up at the foot of the precipice,
where it is evident they have fallen from the dizzy
height, and the descending torrent dashes against
them and flashes up in foam and spray.

This of itself will afford ample study for the forenoon.

In the afternoon, proceeding again to Prospect Park,
ride down the Inclined Railway and take a trip on the
little steamer " Maid of the Mist."

TRIP ON (Charge, 50 cents each person.)
Before you are aware of it, you
" MAID OF THE find yourself in the middle of the
MIST." stream, and the boat riding gracefully over the heavy swells. What
a scene now courts your eager gaze : the mighty cataract in all its sublimity and immensity is above and
before you.

You are in the nave of a vast temple, whose walls
seem the eternal hills, corniced with crags, ornamented
with a fretwork of trees, shrubs, flowers, and foliage;
whose dome is the blue heaven, and whose altar is the
mighty cataract, draped with hangings of green and
snow, while from its unseen base clouds of incense are
ascending to the skies, and bearing up the solemn peal
of its mist-hidden thunder-toned organ. The floor is
of emerald and alabaster; elements are the ministers,
and you a worshiper. This temple was the work of
Nature, and to the God of Nature erected. Human
hands could not lift even a corner of its veil; human

18

art could not equal the smallest of its marvels; human eyes could not penetrate the least of its mysteries.

A vast semi-circle of cataracts stretches around you, forming a scene of surpassing splendor and sublimity. Huge and massy walls of rock are on either side, and the shivering boat in which you sit, floats upon the surface of a sea, fathomless, convulsed, and immeasurable. Endless torrents, bursting as it were from the opened heavens, leap from the brow of the tremendous precipice, plunge headlong down the terrific height, and lash the deep profound, into which they are hurled, to foam and madness. The sonorous breathings of the tortured abyss roll up and reverberate in thunder-peals; and air and earth tremble at the shock of the contending floods. Dense clouds of spray, rolling and curling up in shapeless and ever-varying forms, conceal the meeting of the waters, and majestically soar aloft, heaven-borne on the wings of the wind. The sun, shedding refulgent splendors upon the glorious scene, seems girdled with a radiant halo by the rising mists; and rainbows, broken into fragments by the shifting vapors, appear and vanish, dazzle and dissolve, on every side, in quick and magic succession.

WEDNESDAY.

In the morning visit Goat Island, lingering in the forest walk directly through the heart of the Island, and leading to the romantic beauties of the Three Sister Islands.

In the afternoon take the still more beautiful walk through Goat Island to the entrance to the stair-case leading to the Cave of the Winds. You will there be furnished with a guide and an oil-skin suit, and descend the stair-case and follow the bank to the Lunar Falls, under which is situate the Cave of the Winds.

There is no more exciting and exhilarating excursion to be made at the Falls than that through the Cave

of the Winds. Nowhere else are the rainbow hues
exhibited in such wonderful variety, nor in such surpassing brilliancy and beauty. Rainbow-spray, rain-
bow-dust, and shattered rainbows are scattered around;
rainbow-bars, and arches, horizontal and perpendicular,
are flashing and forming, breaking and re-forming
around and above in the most fantastic and delightful
confusion. The young husband may literally place his
charming bride in a living sparkling rainbow frame,
flecked all over with diamonds and pearls.

Let us now describe the experience more in detail.
Descend the sloping bank to the Lower Fishing Rock
— as a limestone mass, at the l west point of the island
shore, is called — from whence the best view of the
American Falls is presented, that can be anywhere obtained, unless, perhaps, from the river directly in front
of it. The whole beautiful cascade
hangs like a flashing curtain of
shifting snow-wreaths before you,
waving in fleecy folds, and pillared
by downy columns of the softest,
clearest white; around and over all
of which a genial glory seems to float, bright and pure
as the hope and faith of an angel-choir. The scene is
lovely beyond all conception. Nothing on earth can
compare in that respect with the American Fall, as seen
from this spot. Vast as it is, you do not observe its size;
lofty as it is, you take no note of its height; august as
it is, you scarcely perceive its grandeur; — its surpassing
loveliness, and transcendant beauty alone seem to en-
gage your attention. Finally, however, all these become
blended together, and you begin to realize the majesty,
as well as the loveliness, the sublimity, as well as the
beauty of this incomparable cascade, and to feel that
the power as well as the goodness of the Divine Archi-
tect has here its lasting and visible impress. Long will
that glorious scene live in our memory, hallowed by the
recollection of a holy rapture, and an earnest worship.

VISIT TO
"CAVE OF THE
WINDS."

Re-ascend the sloping bank to the Central Fall, and the Cave of the Winds is before you. At the entrance you pause to look up at the projecting cliff, and the sparkling torrent that shoots off far above, falling far over, and far below you; and down at the piles of rock heaped up around, and the foam and spray springing to light and loveliness from the rock-wave concussion. The mightiest throes give birth to the most beautiful things; and thus the rainbow was born of the deluge.

You are on the steps descending into the cavern. The majesty, the sublimity of the scene cannot escape your notice, and you will feel what I find it impossible to express. A wall of rock rises frowning on one side; the falling sheet arches the other. You see it leap from the cliff far above, and lash the rocks far below. You seem between two eternities, with a great mystery before you, whose secrets are about to be revealed. What a moment is this! From the vast cavern into which you are passing comes the sound of a thousand storms. You hear the mad winds raging around the walls of their imprisonment, and mingling their fearful roar with the reverberating thunders of the cataract. The spray falls thick around you; almost overpowered with intense emotion, you hasten on, descend the steps, reach the bottom, instinctively retire from the rushing waters, and, having gained the centre and back of the cave, pause to look around. You seem all eyes, all ears, all soul. You are in the sublime sanctuary of nature; her wonderful and fearful mysteries are above, beneath, and around you. God is Infinite, you are nothing. This is His temple, you are His worshiper. It is impossible in such a place to be irreverent. The proudest here is meek; the haughtiest, humble; and the loftiest, lowly.

Between the Central and American Falls, and at the foot of Luna Island, there is a narrow vacant space, bounded and almost overarched by the tumbling torrent, from which grand views are presented of these two cascades — that of the latter is particularly fine. Here you may rest yourself, or ramble over the huge rocks, in the pure air, with the bright river and the blessed sky before you, and the dark rock above, and then pass under the American sheet as far as you desire, or dare. It is a frightful place, overwhelming in its gloom, grandeur, and sublimity; and there be few who have ventured far, though it is supposed possible to pass quite through and under the whole vast cascade.

THURSDAY.

In the morning visit the upper end of Goat or Iris Island taking with you an interesting and inspiring book, alternately reading and sight-seeing until noon.

You see the broad river spread out before you like a shining sea, with Schlosser on the left, Chippewa far off to the right, and Grand, Navy, and other islands in the dim distance above. It was here, and near the old log upon which you are probably now sitting, that visitors to Iris Island were landed from boats, before the bridge was built. Such was then the only mode of reaching it, and the passage required great care, skill, and exertion, and was, of course, expensive. The island was therefore, at that time, a *terra incognita* to most persons — an unattainable object of intense desire. They could see that it was beautiful, that it presented grand views of the sublime cataract they had come from afar to behold; but alas! they could not set foot upon its velvet surface, repose beneath its shady groves, nor witness from its banks the marvelous glories that clustered around it, and in the midst of which it so sweetly slumbered. Happy traveler! you can pass when you please, see all that it has to reveal, and ramble over and about it at your leisure.

VISIT TO

HEAD OF GOAT

ISLAND.

GOAT ISLAND TERRAPIN ROCKS AND UPPER RIVER

In the afternoon proceed down the street leading to Prospect Park and just at the entrance by the soldiers' monument turn to the right and in a moment you will reach the new Suspension Bridge. Mr. W. D. Howells has so well described the view here that it will bear repetition. Read it as you stand on the bridge. You will find it just, adequate, and true. Here it is :

" Over the river, so still with its oily eddies and delicate wreaths of foam, just below the Falls they have woven a web of wire high in air and hung a bridge from precipice to precipice. Of all the bridges made with hands it seems the lightest, most ethereal; it is ideally graceful and droops from its slight towers like a garland. It is worthy to command the whole grandeur of Niagara and to show the traveler the vast spectacle, with all the awful pomp of the rapids, the solemn darkness of the wooded islands, the mystery of the vaporous gulf, the indomitable wildness of the shores, as far as the eye can reach up or down the fatal stream. The last hues of sunset lingered in the mists that sprung from the base of the Falls with a mournful tremulous grace and a movement weird as the play of the northern lights. They were touched with the most delicate purples and crimsons that darkened to deep red and then faded from them on a second look and they flew upward, swiftly upward, like troops of pale transparent ghosts; while a perfectly clear radiance dwelt upon the scene. Far under the bridge the river smoothly swam, the under currents smoothly unfolding themselves with a vast rose like evolution edged all round with faint lines of white, where the air that filled the water freed itself in foam. What had been clear green on the face of the cataract was here more like rich verd-antique and had a look of firmness almost like that of stone itself. In front where tumbled rocks and expanses of

VIEW FROM NEW SUSPENSION BRIDGE.

23

naked clay varied the gloomier and gayer green, sprung
those spectral mists; and through them loomed out
in its manifold majesty Niagara, with the seemingly
immovable white Gothic screen of the American Fall
and the green massive curve of the Horseshoe, solid
and simple and calm as an Egyptian wall; while beyond this, with their white and black expanses broken
by dark foliaged little isles, the steep Canadian rapids
billowed themselves down between their heavily wooded
shores. The wedding journeyers hung, they knew
not how long, in rapture on the sight."

The expense of crossing over and back for each person is 25 cents, and when on the Canadian side, turn to
the left, up the river bank and in a few steps you are
in the Queen Victoria Jubilee Park, extending from the
upper Suspension Bridge to far above the Horseshoe
Fall. This park is entirely free, and is the property of
the Canadian government. It
is thus described in the official
pamphlet issued by the park
commissioners:

QUEEN VICTORIA
JUBILEE PARK.

The Queen Victoria Niagara Falls Park covers an
area of about 154 acres. It extends along the western
bank of the Niagara a distance of 2½ miles; the width
embraces all the land lying between the water's edge
and the steep wooded bluff, which forms a magnificent
natural boundary on the west. Midway between the
two ends there is a finely wooded island, whose shores
wage never-ceasing conflict with the impetuous waters,
a moment before they plunge into the abyss. From the
pathway on this (Cedar) island good views are obtained
of the whole reach of the rapids above the cataract.
Near the southern end of the park, nestling in a deep
indentation of the shore, is a group of islands, re-named
in honor of Lord Dufferin, which are wondrously beautiful. Pretty rustic bridges connect these islets, and
sylvan rambles and bowers have been provided so that
visitors may enjoy nature, in some of its most charming

24

forms, with comfort and ease. Between Cedar Island and the Dufferin Islands, the Grand Rapids drive affords a continuous view of the tumbling waters as they leap from ledge to ledge down the 55 or 56 feet of descent, between the level of smooth water and the crest of the great fall. Altogether this is one of the most impressive sights to be had, and is second only to the views of the great cataract itself. A fine commanding view is obtained from the top of the bluffs, beyond the Dufferin Islands, termed "Prospect Drive;" it is well worth visiting, as from it you overlook the whole sweep of the river from Navy Island to the gorge below the falls. The immediate locality of the falls is remarkable for the richness of its flora, and many hundreds of varieties of flowering and fern-like plants, growing without cultivation, are to be found within the limits of the park.

All along the bank of the river from the Bridge toward Table Rock the best and grandest of all the upper views of the Falls is presented.

The eye here grasps at a glance the whole mighty measure of the cataract; and Niagara in all its beauty and glory, in all its majesty and immensity, is spanned by a single look. It is before you, revealed in all its grandeur and extent, in all its splendor and sublimity. You stand entranced and spell-bound. Amazement and admiration are in your gaze; awe and reverence in your soul. It is a scene to linger on, and long you linger, turning often away to rest the eye, and relieve the mind, and as often recurring to it with increased wonder and interest. VIEW FROM But at length you pass on, with it still TABLE ROCK. in your eye and mind, to Table Rock, which at length you reach. The view of the Horseshoe Fall from this point is indeed magnificent.

No wonder that the scene from Table Rock has been lauded and extolled. No wonder that it has been

25

the *ultima thule* of many a long and weary pilgrimage.
It is all that has been said of it, and infinitely more —
words cannot convey an idea of its unearthly sublimity
and grandeur. The sea of rapids leaping and tossing
above; the vast breadth and depth of the raging
stream; the impetuous rush of the ocean-torrent; the
awful plunge of the prodigious volume; the tremendous concussion, heard and felt, but not seen from the
covering mists that envelop and hide the crushing
appulsion of the meeting masses; the pointed spear-
shaped jets that shoot up from the convulsed bosom of
the heaving and surging abyss; the multitudinous
whirling, shifting, convolving clouds of spray and
vapor that roll heavily up and load the unresting air;
the dark, threatening cliffs that shut in the vexed and
foam-covered accumulation of floods, in the angry gulf
below; the resplendent glories shed over all by the
burning sun, tinting with gorgeous colors the sheet, the
stream, and the spray, wreathing with rainbow hues
the fleecy and emerald robes of the grand cascade and
arching the fearful chasm with a zone of brightness and
beauty; the wild hoarse roar of the mad rapids, and
the deep booming thunders of the cloud-compelling
cataracts — these, and a thousand other collateral and
subordinate features, combine to form a scene which
appals and confounds the observer, while it attracts
and rivets his wrapt and eager gaze. God of Omnipotence! this wonder is Thy work; the very ground is
holy with Thy presence! This you feel — must feel —
though, perhaps, you do not speak it. Crowding emotions swell the bosom; thoughts that defy utterance fill
the mind. The power and presence of the Almighty
seem fearfully manifest. You gaze, and tremble as you
gaze!

Table Rock is on the same level with the Fall, and
is a continuation of the ledge or strata from which the
torrent-flood is precipitated. It projects over the bank
and beyond the curve of the cascade to a considerable

ry pilgrimage.
itely more —
thly sublimity
g and tossing
f the raging
n-torrent; the
; the tremen-
seen from the
the crushing
ointed spear-
lsed bosom of
multitudinous
of spray and
unresting air:
the vexed and
the angry gulf
ver all by the
; the sheet, the
rainbow hues
d cascade and
brightness and
ad rapids, and
ud-compelling
collateral and
a scene which
hile it attracts
od of Omnip-
very ground is
— must feel —
crowding unio-
fy utterance fill
f the Almighty
tremble as you

h the Fall, and
from which the
s over the bank
a considerable

distance, and from this circumstance derives its name, having in some respects a tabular aspect. Creep to the edge and look down—the sensation is awful. There is nothing but the invisible and imponderable air between the thin leaf-like crag which supports you and the massy blocks of limestone that lay concentrated more than one hundred feet beneath, where they have fallen from the dizzy elevation whence you look, and been rent and scattered by the shock. There is a strange and indefinable fascination in the terrible depth that confronts you,

"Charming the eye with dread ; "

and it requires an effort to withdraw from that horrible verge of danger and death.

Having now admired the scene for sufficient length of time to desire reluctantly to abandon it, and resolving to return again, proceed a short distance above Table Rock, when you will be, if you desire, accommodated with guide and suit to go in under the Canadian Falls.

TRIP UNDER THE CANADIAN FALLS.

You soon arrive at the misty, spray-washed entrance to the cavern, which it is your purpose to explore. Here you pause to enjoy a most sublime view of the cataract, and particularly of the Horseshoe Fall, which comes thundering down, above and before you, stretching far away to the left in its huge and awful proportions. Another, and in some respects, a better view of the same grand spectacle, is seen from the river margin to which you descend.

From this point, more than any other, you appear to realize the vast height of the precipice, and the prodigious weight and impulsion of the torrent. It seems a god-hurled flood, and you an insect atom, scarce beyond its rush. Tremendous in its force, immense in its extent, appalling in its sublimity, the vast cascade

27

confounds and terrifies you, while it holds your gaze
with a charm you can neither comprehend nor break.
A dread indefinable divinity is in and upon it, which
compels your adoration of Him who piled the rock,
and heaved the flood that made Niagara, and made it
speak of Him, through every sense of power and beauty,
to mind and soul. There is a god-ness in the scene,
that is felt in every fibre, but cannot be expressed,—
that infinitely expands the soul, which is yet too small
to grasp its dim outline even,—that crowds the mind
with august thoughts and emotions, which struggle
for utterance, but which the heart only can tell to its
Creator in the silent eloquence of worship.

Of all views of Niagara, this is the most impressive; and, were there no other, it would seem inexplicable from whence these unintermitted and immeasurable floods could proceed, which appear literally to fall
from the heavens. From this scene, tearing yourself
away, you regain the top of the sloping bank, and im-
patient to attain the penetralia of nature's hidden mysteries, essay the passage behind the sheet. The winds
howl around you; — the spray dashes in your face
with blinding and almost suffocating force. You can
scarcely see, scarcely breathe; but the supporting hand
of the guide, and his encouraging voice sustain and
re-assure you. With hasty but careful steps you pass
on, and are in a moment more, at your journey's end,
and can both see and breathe more freely. The spray
still showers upon you, but with diminished force and
density; and you look around, above, below. What
a fearful place! what an imposing scene! unutterable
awe is the first, and for some seconds the only
emotion.

You stand upon a narrow ledge, scarce three feet
wide, and gaze with intense interest up ninety feet at
the meeting arches of rock and water; and down
seventy feet at a steep precipice, and a flashing sheet,
which are lost to view in the rising mists. You see

the mighty torrent roll off the cliffs above your head, and plunge with a lightning rapidity, down the dark profound. You cannot see the strife between fall and flood — the mad mêlée of many waters; — but you hear the sound of the battling elements, and you feel that the struggle is terrific. Such sights! such sounds! — The eye aches; the ear is pained. But there is a dreadful fascination in the place: — the eye looks eagerly, though it aches; and the ear is pleased with that which pains it.

An inviting extent of cavern, dim, misty, and indefinable, is before you. You long to explore it, and advance a step, when the guide, catching your arm, assures you that you stand upon the extremity of Termination Rock, and that, though it is possible to make your way a few feet further, the attempt would be at the hazard of your life. Reluctantly you abandon the hope of diving still deeper into the shadowy recesses of that terribly attractive cavern, and survey with a closer scrutiny the vaulted hall in which you stand. Ragged, impending, and seamed with fissures, the arching rock above you appears to be on the point of crumbling beneath the weight of the superincumbent flood. Massy fragments, held by no visible support, seem almost in the act of falling, and you can hardly persuade yourself that danger is not imminent and destruction at hand. But the reflection that thousands and thousands of persons have passed under them, back and forth, with impunity, inspires you with courage, and you scan, but with a throbbing pulse and a heaving bosom, the wonders and glories by which you are surrounded.

The living deluge that bursts from the trembling crag above you, and flashing by is scarcely seen ere it thunders up from the gulf below, seems to make an eternal present of both past and future, by its lightning rush and ceaseless flow. Omnipotence mingling infinities, dashing down the flood, lifting the spray, and

swelling the sound, pervades the place with His presence, and deepens the awe it inspires. But any
attempt to describe the sights, sounds, or sensations
produced by this transcendent scene must be vain, and
worse than vain; and I leave you "amid these vast and
eternal workings of gigantic Nature" to commune
with Him, "whom Nature's self obeys," and remain or
emerge at will.

FRIDAY.

Taking your lunch with you proceed to the New
York Central depot, and at 9, or 10, or 11 o'clock —
for the train runs every hour — take the trip to Lewiston by train, and to Fort Niagara on the steamer, and
return in time for dinner in the evening. The expense
of the entire trip is but 50 cents. It is
TRIP TO   replete with interest, beauty and grand-
LEWISTON,   eur, and is in effect a complete view of
lower Niagara, from the cataract to Lake
Ontario. Well may one exclaim :

"Majestic stream ! what river rivals thee,
  Thou child of many lakes and sire of one —
Lakes that claim kindred with the all-circling sea —
  Large at thy birth as when thy race is run :
Against what great obstructions hast thou won
  Thine august way — the rock-formed mountain-plain
Has opened at thy bidding, and the steep
  Bars not thy passage, for the ledge in vain
Stretches across the channel — thou dost leap
Sublimely down the height, and urge again
Thy rock-embattled course on to the distant main."

Niagara River is, indeed, in its whole course, quite
in keeping with the stupendous cataract from which its
principal interest is derived. There is nothing insig-
nificant, nothing paltry, nothing common-place about
it, from the lake in which its vast floods have birth, to
that which they supply. It is everywhere grand,
mighty, and majestic. When spread to the dimensions

GREAT ICE MOUNTAIN

of a little sea, it has no resemblance to a shoal; and when contracted to the breadth of a creek, it seems to possess the power of an ocean. The very interruptions it meets with in its way, seemed placed there only to exhibit the immensity of its force. The basin which receives its prodigious far-falling volume, resembles an abyss without bounds to its capacity; the compressed channel through which it then flows, seems to have opened its rock and banks to an imprisoned sea, that would have burst a passage, had escape been denied.

Making a sharp angle at the Falls, it rolls on through beautiful curves in an almost straight direction for about two miles, then winds gracefully off to the left, and passing through a succession of noble bends, rushes, wild, impetuous, and uncontrollable, into the Whirlpool, where, like a baffled Titan, struggling with his bonds, it rages and plunges round the impenetrable barriers that hem it in; and at last, having gathered anew its mighty energies, rushes headlong on in a fresh direction, and bounds away, free, fearless, and triumphant.

Continuing in its new course — having turned less than a right-angle — but a short distance, it rolls away gradually to the west, and having regained its former direction, hurries on, inclining now to the right, and again bending to the left, here maddened by restraint, and there soothed by expansion, to the end of the mountain plain, from the gaping jaws of which it rushes angrily forth, but soon recovering the serenity of its native seas, and no longer chafed or enraged, it flows quietly and smoothly on, through gentle curves and wooing banks, to the sweet lake whose soft embrace it has come so far and encountered so much to meet, and in whose peaceful bosom it finally sinks to repose.

From the foot of the mountain ridge to Lake Ontario nothing can be more lovely than this river. It is a rapture to look upon its bright and tranquil course. It glides along so silently and almost imperceptibly, its surface is so calm and glassy, its breadth so uniform and expansive, its water so clear and deep, its banks so smooth and regular, its curvatures so gradual and alternate, its whole aspect so pleasing and harmonious, that a delicious languor steals over the mind, the spirit yields itself unconsciously to a sweet oblivion of turbulence and strife, and its contemplations are of sunny skies, shining streams, and shady groves. The eye lingers with delight upon the blended hues, the graceful turns, and emerald shores of the no longer agitated, but now beautiful, Niagara; and the soul, at peace with itself, with nature, and with all things, indulges in a dreaming delirium of joy, unshadowed by care, untinged with gloom, and unbroken by tumult.

SATURDAY.

Take your lunch with you and then enter the street cars, which start directly opposite the International Café, at the Soldiers' Monument, and which also stop opposite the Spencer House, and you can ride to the lower Suspension Bridge for 5 cents. Cross the bridge to Canada (over and return, 25 cents), and you can easily procure a carriage to take your party for a dollar to the Whirlpool. The cost of entering the enclosure is 50 cents per person. Remain there all the morning. You will find the time all too short.

THE WHIRLPOOL AND WHIRLPOOL RAPIDS.

In the afternoon pass the time delightfully until sundown at the Whirlpool Rapids (entrance to enclosure and down the inclined railway, 50 cents). Here there are lovely walks and shady bowers.

Though all the surrounding country may be melting in fervid heat you will here invariably enjoy a delightful breeze and a most refreshing coolness.

32

The river at the Whirlpool, makes an acute angle in its course, turning abruptly off to the right, behind the cliff upon which you stand. The furious torrent comes thundering and foaming into this great basin; and its currents kept away from the place of egress by the mighty rocks upon which the cliff rests, are forced, by their prodigious impulsion, quite across the mouth of the outlet; and, meeting the opposite bank, are again diverted from their course; and, curving inward, are carried round and round the basin, till they are drawn down in the centre, driven subterraneously far forward, and finally ejected at the opening below, where they boil up, and bound away in frightful and tremendous plunges.

Nothing that has life floats upon this chaos of convulsions; but huge timbers, and sometimes dead bodies, are drawn into its vortex, and carried round in ceaseless gyrations for days, and even weeks, before they escape from its convolving currents, and whirling eddies.

From the height whereon you stand but little of the terrible agitation and wild intumescence of the Whirlpool, can be perceived by the unassisted eye. The little sticks — as they appear to be — which you observe whirling and tossing about, are in reality large pieces of timber; as by the aid of an object glass, you will become convinced and be also enabled to realize something more of the grandeur and commotion of this strange and fearful sea of imprisoned, but rebellious and still raging floods.

By an excellent inclined railway you descend to the base of the cliff, and from the level rocks below observe the wild rush and whirl of the mad waters. The rapids above, and at the entrance of the Whirlpool, are terribly grand and striking. The huge surges leap and plunge with prodigious force and velocity; and their impulsion is so great, that the whole mass is heaved up at the centre of this mighty maelstrom, to an elevation of not less than twelve feet above its outer surface.

Passing round to the right, you come to the outlet of this tumultuous sea, and behold a scene of surpassing grandeur. Two black and frowning cliffs, scarcely thirty rods apart, rear their huge and giant forms to a height of nearly three hundred feet; and there stand, terrible and impending — the mountain-sized, rock-armed guardians of this maelstrom-portal. The escaping torrents, crowding through the narrow passage, and hurrying down the slope, rush forward with such inconceivable rapidity and force, that the middle of the gushing volume is raised much higher than the side next you, which is smooth and glassy, but incredibly swift; and the bounding surges leap away in sublime plunges of eight or ten feet high. These rapids are seen to much better advantage from the opposite side, as they are nearest that shore, and indeed dash along the huge rocks by which it is lined, in their curveting and uncontrollable course.

Nothing that comes down the river can escape being drawn into the Whirlpool, as the current is carried quite across the outlet, and turned up by the opposing bank. Wave urges wave, current accelerates current, billow chases billow, and there they revolve round and round, till, swallowed in one place, ejected in another, contending here, and separating there, parting, reposing, meeting, mingling, eddying, plunging, they at last plunge in the deeps of the abyss, far under the superincumbent mass, and thence emerge at the narrow outlet, whence they hasten away in the mad rapture of new-found freedom, to seek repose in the quiet bosom of the distant lake.

It is utterly impossible to describe the Whirlpool, so as to give any adequate idea of its grandeur and sublimity. Beauty it has none. — It is fearful, terrible. There is not a winning feature about it. It is solemn, awful, impressive; and, as a great natural

curiosity, second only to the mighty cataract of
Niagara.

A visit to the Whirlpool should never be omitted.
It is in all respects totally different from everything
about the Falls. A vast unity of factious and warring
energies, shut in and imprisoned by massy and cloud-
reaching barriers, having no relation or likeness to
aught else in the material world, it is alone in its solemn
strangeness, and touches no chord of human sympathy.
The only emotions it excites are unmitigated astonishment, and inexplicable awe ; — such, at least, was its
effect upon the writer.

The same cause that makes the waters in the basin
below the Falls rise sometimes so quickly, and to such
a height — contraction of the channel — produces a
similar effect in this. A heavy wind down the lake,
raising the river one or two feet, causes it to rise there
from fifteen to twenty feet, and in the Whirlpool to
nearly the same height. At such a time, when it has
received the tribute of destruction, and planks, timbers,
trees, and it may be boats, and dead bodies, are caught
and enveloped in its tremendous toils, it is seen in its
most sublime and awful aspect, and seems, in its wild
delight, a living but imprisoned desolation, sporting
with, while it rends its prey, and yet wearing a savage
solemnity of countenance, in the highest degree hideous
and appalling. At a lower stage of water, its currents,
cavities, eddies, gyrations, are more distinctly marked,
and the view, though less striking, is perhaps more impressive. Seen at any time, and seen aright, it cannot
fail to excite astonishment, and fill the soul with awe.

A large raft of timber escaped some years since
from its fastenings above the Falls, and was precipitated over the cataract. The disjoined logs were
speedily hurried to the Whirlpool, in which they re-
mained for a number of weeks. It then presented a
scene, as those who beheld it relate, of intense and
startling interest. Scattered about in every direction,

they were to be seen in all attitudes, and from listless
inanity, to a wonderful life-likeness. Some were
floating on the glassy surface, others riding the gentle
swells, some careering over the rolling hillows, and
again others leaping, wrestling, crashing, plunging,
flying, following, retreating, pursuing, shooting up high
in the air, diving far down in the deep, hiding here,
and starting up there, as if a mad forest of trees, riding
these infernal surges, beh-' here a wild inebriate revel —
or rather as if the mob of waters, seizing these immense
weapons, waged intestine war, and fought one another
— flood threshing flood, and surge goading surge with
these Titanic war-clubs, now mingling in the horrid
mêlée of strife, now thrown far apart, and again rushing together, implacable, vindictive, and unrelenting.
It must have been a strange and fearful scene.

SUNDAY.

Excellent churches, Episcopalian, Presbyterian, Meth-
odist, and Koman Catholic are in the village, and as
this is a day of r st, no trip is proposed. Your mind
if you have properly studied Niagara, will be in a deeply
reverential mood and you will be prepared to say of the
different views of Niagara, what Thompson in his beautiful hymn says of the seasons.

These as they change, Almighty Father, these
Are but the varied God I The rolling year
Is full of Thee. Forth in the pleasing spring
Thy beauty walks, Thy tenderness and love.
Wide flush the fields; the softening air is balm
And every sense and every heart is joy.
Then comes Thy glory in the summer months.
Thy bounty shines in Autumn unconfined
And spreads a common feast for all that lives.
In Winter, awful Thou I With clouds and storms
Around Thee thrown, tempest o'er tempest rolled
Majestic darkness I on the whirlwind's wing
Riding sublime, Thou bidst the world adore.

36

nd from listless
. Some were
ding the gentle
g billows, and
ing. plunging,
rooting up high
p. hiding here,
of trees, riding
ebriate revel —
these immense
ht one another
ling surge with
; in the horrid
nd again rush-
d unrelenting.
scene.

oyterian, Meth-
village, and as
. Your mind
l be in a deeply
d to say of the
on in his beau-

, these
ar
spring
love.
is balm

ionths.
d
lives.
nd storms
est rolled
ing
dure.

In the evening. if you are fortunate enough to visit Niagara during the full moon, it will surely not be impious to visit Luna Island and behold the scene spiritualized by the lunar bow.

There is a witching loveliness about this island in the soft obscurity of evening that cannot fail to please ; and a solemn grandeur in the cataract at night that commands reverence. Then, too, imagination holds her undisputed sway ; but the half-concealment that shrouds every object, confines her to the task of filling up the shadowy **THE** outline of the vast indistinct, that is **LUNAR BOW.** everywhere around. It seems a spirit-land, and gigantic forms of essential grace and beauty float before the vision, upon the atmosphere of fancy. Hushed is the voice of mirth, silent the tongue of conviviality. The actual blends with the ideal ; contemplation rules the hour and the place, and a subdued, but not dismal, melancholy pervades every brow and bosom. No sound is heard but the choral chant of the elements ; no sentiment breathed but such as befits the spot and the season. The Genus of Niagara, hovering near, spreads his misty pinions over all things, and the whole scene is hallowed by the invisible presence of Deity.

MONDAY.

Walk across the upper Suspension Bridge (toll over and back, 25 cents), and engaging a carriage on the other side, drive to the Dufferin Isles (entrance for the entire party in a double carriage, 50 cents). Take your lunch with you, let your carriage go, directing it to call for you at five o'clock in the evening. You will pass here one of the most delightful days in your life. You will never forget their wild and romantic beauties, their quiet and shady bowers, their virginal freshness and sweetness ; and having gone once — many days will be

37

passed there in blessed rest and peace. Mr. Charles Dudley Warner in " Their Pilgrinage," describes one of the views therefrom.

" In the afternoon, under a broken sky, the rapids above the Horseshoe reminded one of the seashore on a very stormy day; impeded by the rocks, the flood hesitated, and even ran back, as if reluctant to take the final plunge. The sienna color of the water on the table contrasted sharply with the emerald on the brink of the Fall. The rainbow, springing out of the center of the caldron, arched clear over the American Cataract, and was one moment bright, and the next dimly seen through the mist which boiled up out of the foam of waters and swayed in the wind. Through this veil darted adventurous birds, flashing their wings in the prismatic colors, and circling about as if fascinated by the awful rush and thunder. With the shifting wind and the passing clouds, the scene was in perpetual change — now, the American Fall was creamy white, and the mist below, dark; and again, the heavy mass was gray and sullen, and the mist like silver spray. Perhaps nowhere else in the world is the force of Nature so overpowering to the mind, and, as the eye wanders from the chaos of the Fall to the far horizon, where the vast rivers of rapids are poured out of the sky, one feels that this force is inexhaustible and eternal."

VIEW FROM THE DUFFERIN ISLES.

TUESDAY.

Take a carriage and drive down the bank of the river *along the American side,* taking your lunch, stopping at that most interesting historical locality, the Bloody Run; thence to the heights above Lewiston, commanding a most magnificent view of the windings of t e river and the lovely valley of the lower Niagara and of

38

SPENCER HOUSE

Lake Ontario, returning to the Hotel for dinner at six (cost of carriage for one or more, six dollars; no tolls).

WEDNESDAY.

In the morning walk about the State Park along the bank to the upper rapids, lingering on the way to obtain many beautiful views of the river.

In the afternoon drive along the upper r   on the American side, to La Salle, through a most delightful section of country, and in full view of the river. (Cost of drive, four dollars for carriage for party.)

THURSDAY.

Take a carriage, having your lunch with you, and drive on the Canadian side to the historic battle-field of Queenstown and the monument erected to General Brock at Queenstown Heights. This is, in its historical features, one of the most interesting trips at the Falls, and the outlook from the Heights is grand. (Carriage for entire day for party of five, seven dollars.)

FRIDAY.

After the long drive of Thursday you will find it most restful to read or sit upon the cool piazza of the Hotel, or make, possibly, a short visit to Prospect Park, the afternoon being passed in writing to your friends about the many charming experiences you have had and the benefit of these suggestions, a copy of which you may obtain free at the office, and enclose to your friends.

SATURDAY.

Take a carriage and your lunch, and cross the New Suspension Bridge to visit Lundy's Lane battle grounds, passing thence to what is unquestionably the most beautiful drive about Niagara, viz.: the Canadian river bank up to the village of Chippewa, and thence to the

upper river, commanding a wide prospect of the islands,
and returning thence through the Dufferin Islands.
(Expense of carriage per day for party, six dollars.)
No extra charge is made at the hotels named above
for putting up lunches for guests.

Of course, these suggestions could be greatly ex-
tended by the details of trips upon the upper river,
where there is even better fishing than at the Thousand
Islands.

Of course, too, each of the spots above named can
and will be visited more than once, and with a day's
rest between passed in the commodious and comfortable rooms of your hotel.

It should also be borne in mind that upon the visits
to the Whirlpool and Whirlpool Rapids, Islands, Canadian side, Queen Victoria Park, Dufferin Islands, much
cheaper means of transportation than carriages is
offered by the street railways and vans, which are not
so exclusive, but fairly comfortable, and much less
expensive.

And now, reader, you have, I trust, begun fairly to
appreciate the power, majesty, and beauty of Niagara.
Do you know a more delightful place in which to pass
the summer? Can you find elsewhere — to speak first
of mere material wants — air more pure, water more
limpid, drainage more perfect, climate more delightful?
Do you know of any other spot which so exalts the
imagination, stimulates the intellect, deepens the feel-
ings of reverence and awe, and which so exhilarates
with the sweetness and rapture inspired by scenes of
exquisite natural beauty?
Believe me, dear reader, when I tell you that you
have not begun to yet understand it. "Age cannot

wither nor repetition stale its infinite variety." It is forever fair, forever new. In the wild confusion - the fierce competition of business — you may think of its tossing rapids and its impetuous hurrying stream; in your moments of darkness and despair you may, perhaps, dwell on its lonely and terrible Whirlpool ; in your moments of anger, or bitterness, or envy, the fierce force and terrific power of its awful plunge may be before you; but again and again, after all these are gone will arise in the mind's eye, that eternal image of majesty, power, sweetness, purity, and beauty — the limpid waters of the great cataract, falling, falling forever in unending *peace* — yet falli.,, only to rise again spiritualized, chastened, in the spray floating away to heaven. And behold! — on the dazzling bosom of that spirit-shape, God's own bow of promise — the lasting image of hope, of goodness, of pardon and reconciliation ; far above all strife, and tumult, and pain, this shines and will in the blessed sunlight shine forever!

Such are the scenes, Niagara, that make us love thee, and bind us year after year with unabated affection to thy shores.

And yet, year after year, thousands will come from the fens and marshes of the sea, from the depressing outlook, and the narrow, vacant life of the country village, from the stifling streets and the reeking pavements of the crowded city, and, entering upon thy scenes of loveliness, sweetness and sublimity, will rush madly about and attempt to see and understand thee in a day! "Verily I say unto you, they have their reward." For "having eyes they see not, and having ears they hear not, neither do they understand."

WHERE SHALL WE STAY, AND WHAT WILL IT COST AT NIAGARA?

You will find excellent quarters at Niagara Falls
during the winter, spring, and autumn months at the
SPENCER HOUSE — a cosy, homelike hotel. The in-
ternal arrangements of the hotel combine every advantage of quiet, comfort, and convenience. The rooms
are tastefully and richly furnished and scrupulously
clean, Viands that delight the eye and palate, linen,
china, and silver of unexceptionable quality, servants
ready without impertinence, and prompt without brib-
ery, render it a most agreeable place of entertainment.
Charles Dickens has praised its table, Wilkie Collins
its beds and fine linen, Booth declares it his favorite
hotel, Mojeska, Parepa Rosa, Barrett—that prince and
king of good-fellowship, Chauncey M. Depew,— King
Kalakaua, the Grand Duke Alexis, Bartholdi, and hundreds of others have enjoyed its hospitalities. It is
kept on the American plan from May to November.
Its prices for rooms and board on the first floor are
$4.00 per day per person; on the second floor, $3.50,
and on the third floor, $3.00. From November to May
it is kept on the European plan, with rooms $2.00 per
person per day on the first floor; $1.00 per day per
person on the second and third floors, with meals at
any hour to order. It makes special prices per week
or month for families, and these may be ascertained by
writing to the address "SPENCER HOUSE, NIAGARA
FALLS, N. Y." The visitor will do well to do this, as
to think of remaining less than a week is a great mis-
take.

In summer, the great hotel — the finest at Niagara
— is the INTERNATIONAL. The magnificent summer
home is worthy of a visit for itself. It is four stories

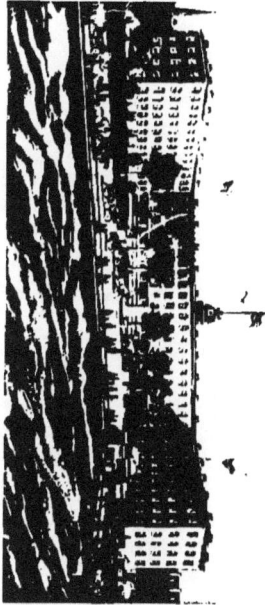

INTERNATIONAL HOTEL

high, built entirely of stone, the kitchens, bakeries, and furnaces are in an entirely distinct building, so that the odor of cookery—to persons of delicate sensibility sometimes, in summer, very offensive—is never present in the very large, spacious, well-ventilated and richly furnished apartments. The hotel faces the new park, and its lawn leads down directly to the rapids. From its magnificent colonnades and rooms an unrivaled view may be had of the American Rapids, and the islands and the brink of the Falls. Indeed, the lawn itself—interspersed with fine beds of beautiful flowers, and with clusters of magnificent forest trees—may be fairly pronounced one of the loveliest spots in the world. Its expanse of verdant grass charms and refreshes the eye; beyond the lawn are the silvery tints, the lustrous white, the indescribable green of the rapids, and the wooded heights of Goat Island—then appear the brink of the cataract, the rising rainbow-tinted spray, and then the rocky shores, the beautiful parks, the forest-crowned hills of Canada "withdrawn afar in time's remotest blue." There is not an object to disturb or annoy, not an unsightly structure to distract the mind, and here for hours, while the happy children play, and the fountain—fresh from Niagara's brink—rises and falls in rhythmic music on the lawn, and the great cataract rests and soothes with its muffled roar softened by distance and alluring to repose—here is the spot to which the traveler may come and find the true fountain of youth for which Ponce de Leon vainly sought in the everglades of the South. No pains are spared to make its table equal to the best hotels in New York City. It is opened from the 15th of June to the 1st of October. Its prices per day are the same as those of the SPENCER HOUSE, and it is kept both upon the American and the European plan. It offers exceptionally low prices to families'. rooms and board on the first floor are $21.00 per week per person; on the second floor $17.50 per week; and on the third floor,

$15.00 per week. As the hotel is fire-proof, with fire-escapes from every room, three stairways, and two elevators, the rooms on the third floor are almost as desirable as those on the first floor. Nurses and children (under 10) are half-price. To secure early choice of rooms it would be well to write not later than June 1st, and it is believed that the traveling public will find the proprietor and all his assistants worthy, efficient and obliging. Letters should be addressed to the INTERNATIONAL HOTEL, NIAGARA FALLS, N. Y.

with fire-
two ele-
lmost as
and chil-
ly choice
han June
will find
efficient
l to the
N. Y.

www.ingramcontent.com/pod-product-compliance
Lightning Source LLC
Chambersburg PA
CBHW022026080426
42733CB00007B/740